THIS IS THE LAITY

Simplification of 'Christifideles Laici'
an Apostolic Exhortation
with a Foreword by
Cardinal Basil Hume OSB

Text prepared by Philippa Craig

A GRAIL PUBLICATION
1989

ISBN 0 901829 77 3
First published 1989
Reprinted July 1989

Published by The Grail, 125 Waxwell Lane
Pinner, Middx HA5 3ER

Distribution: Fowler Wright Books Ltd
Leominster, Herefords HR6 8DE

CONTENTS

FOREWORD

In 1985, the Extraordinary Synod of Bishops, called to celebrate the twentieth anniversary of the ending of the Second Vatican Council, expressed full confirmation of the teachings of that Council as the way forward for the Church into the next millennium.

At the heart of the discussions at that Synod lay the vision of the Church as 'communio' or 'koinonia'. This 'communio' is our sharing in the life of God. It is also the union we enjoy in virtue of being members of the Body of Christ nourished, as we are, by that life of his, just as the sap from the vine gives life to each of the branches. This reality is expressed and celebrated most especially in the Mass. It is the heart of our Catholic life.

From this communion in the life of God comes our mission. As the baptised we are each sent by God to proclaim his love and truth in our world. This mission entrusted to each is therefore the work of the whole Church, priests and lay people alike.

'Christifideles Laici', to give this document its Latin title, is a wonderful presentation of the role and mission of the lay members of Christ's faithful people. To have studied the Holy Father's Apostolic Letter is to have an understanding and appreciation of the dignity and responsibility which are ours because of our baptism.

The next Synod of Bishops, in 1990, in studying in particular priestly formation, will look at the ways in which the co-operation and partnership of priests and lay people can be improved. The work of these two Synods, taken together, will give us a good practical foundation for our mission as we approach the Decade of Evangelisation (1990 to 2000) called for by the Holy Father.

I thank the Grail for their splendid work in preparing this version of 'Christifideles Laici'. I know you will find it most helpful.

Basil Hume

Cardinal Basil Hume OSB
Archbishop of Westminster

PREFACE

The Vocation and Mission of the Lay Faithful in the Church and in the World was the subject discussed at the 1987 Synod of Bishops. They were profoundly influenced by the many consultations with lay people which took place before the Synod met and by the active participation of lay people within the Synod itself. In addition, the outlook of the Synod Fathers was influenced by the documents that had been issued since the Second Vatican Council and especially by 'Evangelii Nuntiandi' of Pope Paul VI. The fruit of all this work has been distilled in this remarkable document by Pope John Paul II.

Here the parable of the labourers in the vineyard from Matthew's Gospel and that of the vine and the branches from John, as well as many texts relating to Baptism come to life in a new way. We see more clearly our call to proclaim Christ to the world and how essential it is that priests and lay people work together in this great task. At the heart of this work the Pope places our duty 'to rediscover and to make others rediscover the inviolable dignity of every human person' (37).

In **'Christifideles Laici'** we have a programme of formation for all Christians. The Pope insists that 'the lay state of life has its distinctive feature in its secular character' (55). He asks the whole Church to listen to young people and he invites them to listen to the Church. He encourages older people to retain their sense of mission to the world. He calls on the Church to 'stand firmly against all forms of discrimination and abuse of women' (49) and encourages them to take their rightful place in the life of the Church. Underlying all our apostolic work should be respect for the dignity and freedom of every person created by God and redeemed by Christ.

Firmly based on Scripture and the documents of Vatican II, this Apostolic Exhortation will help to guide the Church into the next century. As a guide to Christian living and action it is fitting that it should be issued before the beginning of the Decade of Evangelisation, when it is hoped that many will come to know the love and mercy of Christ. The task of evangelisation requires that every Christian plays his or her part. We therefore commend this document for use in prayer groups, in senior schools, discussion groups and for individual reading.

We thank the Grail, who produced this simplified version, and we hope that it may lead us to a better understanding of the calling and mission of the lay person in the world today.

+Rt Rev Kevin O'Brien
Auxiliary Bishop of Middlesbrough

Department for Mission and Unity
Bishops Conference of England and Wales

INTRODUCTION

1 In 1987
the Synod of Bishops met in Rome
to consider the vocation and mission
of the lay faithful twenty years after
the Second Vatican Council.
One can compare these lay people
to the workers in Matthew's story
of the vineyard,
for this story recalls Christ's vineyard
and the people called to labour in it.
This vineyard is the world,
the world that in God's plan
must be transformed.

'Go into My Vineyard'
2 The vineyard owner saw people standing idle.
He urged them to work, saying:
'You go into the vineyard too'. (Cf Matt.20:3-4)
Since then, the Lord has never ceased
to say the same words.
Bishops, clergy, religious and lay people
are all personally called by Christ
and given a mission
on behalf of the Church and of the world.

Vatican II has written profoundly
about the mission of the laity.
It urged them to respond generously,
and to associate themselves with Christ
in his work of salvation.

Lay people were present at the Synod,
representing the laity of the whole world.
They made a valuable contribution
through their experience,

their suggestions and advice.

Looking back to the time since Vatican II,
the Synod saw clearly
how the Holy Spirit
continues to renew the Church
and to inspire new longings for holiness;
how the Spirit inspires the participation
of so many of the faithful.
This is evident in many fields:
in a new collaboration between priests,
religious and lay people;
in deeper participation in the liturgy,
preaching and teaching;
in the many ministries
and ways of serving in the Church
now entrusted to lay people;
in the flowering of groups
and spiritual movements;
in a lay commitment to the Church's life;
in the increasing participation
of women in society.

At the same time,
these things have brought
their own temptations.
One, is to become so caught up
in Church affairs
as to fail in proper responsibility
for the secular world.
Another, is to justify separating faith and life;
to believe what the Gospel says
rather than to live it out where one is.

The Synod constantly referred back
to Vatican II,
to its prophetic teaching on the laity.
It had the challenge of turning
a rich 'theory'
into concrete ways of expressing it.

Some situations have arisen
since Vatican II
which the Synod has studied carefully.
These are situations concerning
the ministries and church services
entrusted to the laity,
the spread of new movements
alongside other lay groups,
and the place and role of women
in the Church and in society.

TODAY'S URGENT NEEDS

3 The whole point of the Synod,
its chief hope,
is that the lay people
will heed Christ's call
to work in his vineyard,
will become active and responsible workers
in the mission of the Church.

This is particularly urgent today.
New situations are arising
in the Church and in society
and no-one has the right to stay idle.
Matthew's Gospel says
that the vineyard owner
found people standing idle
and sent them into the vineyard
with the others.
Christ speaks the same words to us.
His voice resounds
in each of his followers,
incorporated as we are
as living members of the Church.
Christ also speaks to us
in the events of history.
As Vatican II said,
the People of God moved by faith
try to find signs
of God's presence and purpose

in the events and needs and hopes
which they share with their contemporaries.

The world is changing rapidly.
Still it is possible to highlight
some of the trends that are emerging.
In the Gospel story
the good grain and the weeds
both grew together in the field.
The same is true today:
opposites and contradictions
grow side by side;
good and evil, justice and injustice,
anguish and hope.

Secularism and the Need for Religion
4 It is impossible not to notice
how religious indifference and secularism
are spreading.
People are affected by
scientific achievements
and developments in technology;
and they want no restrictions
on their liberty.
God becomes meaningless for them.
They forget him and begin to adore
other idols offered by today's world.

This is a serious situation.
Not only is it happening to individuals
but to whole communities of people,
even to long-standing Christian peoples.
On the other hand,
no one can totally extinguish
the human longing for religion.
When people are brave enough to face
serious questions on the purpose of life,
about suffering and dying,
then they have to recognise their need
for the God who created them.

The world increasingly recognises this
in an openness to spiritual values,
in a new interest in religious research,
in a return to prayer,
and in demands for religious freedom.

The Human Person

5 When individuals are not seen
as images of God
then they are open to every form of manipulation.
They can be reduced to slavery
by ideologies and economic power,
by political systems,
scientific technocracy
or the intrusiveness of the mass media.
We see women and men
whose rights are being violated
by unjust laws:
their right to life and to integrity,
to a home and to employment,
their right to a family
and responsible parenthood,
their right to take part
in public life,
their right to freedom of conscience
and the practice of religion.

How many abortions have been performed,
how many children abandoned and abused.
In some countries,
whole populations lack home and work
and the essentials for a decent human life.
Great areas of misery and want
exist in and around great cities.
All this has gravely affected
entire groups of human beings.

But in spite of this,
the sacredness of the human person
cannot be wiped out,
no matter how it is devalued and violated,

because it is founded in God,
the Creator and Father.

It is essential to keep on re-affirming
the dignity of the individual person.
There is a growing awareness everywhere
that people are not 'things' to be used
but responsible beings
endowed with conscience and freedom
and tending towards spiritual values.

Today is said to be a time of 'humanism',
but strangely enough,
some types of humanism
end up by destroying the individual.
Other types exalt the individual
to the point of idolatry.
But there is a good and true humanism,
which recognises and fosters
the dignity of the human person.

One of the needs of humanity today
is the growing need for participation.
This is a real sign of the times,
an indication of the spread
of true humanism.
Above all, there is a growing need for women
and young people to participate,
not just in family and academic life,
but in cultural, economic,
social and political areas as well.
To be in the forefront of such development
is to become creators
of a new and more humane society.

Conflict and Peace

6 Today, as perhaps never before,
humanity is caught up in conflict,
in hostility between persons, groups,
nations and blocks of nations.
This flares into violence, terrorism, war,

and makes the whole human family suffer.

On the other hand,
individuals and whole peoples
are longing for peace,
and this longing is impossible to suppress.
Whole peoples suffer and work
to bring about peace and justice.
It is the increased participation
of many people in such efforts
that will make it a reality.
Among those found working for peace today
are many of the lay faithful.

JESUS, HOPE OF HUMANITY

7 What a huge task
is facing the labourers in God's vineyard!
The whole Church is working here:
bishops, priests, deacons,
religious women and men and the laity.
The adverse situations mentioned above
deeply affect the Church
but they do not crush it,
because the Spirit upholds its mission
and gives it life.

No matter how terrible the problems,
the Church knows
that all the good efforts of humanity
find full response
in the person of Jesus,
who redeems us and our world.

The Church knows that Jesus sent it out
to be a sign of unity between people
and between people and God
and as a means of achieving that unity.

So humanity can still hope.
It is Jesus

whom the Church constantly proclaims;
Jesus who is himself the Good News.

In this proclamation
the laity have their role.
It is a role that only they can play.
Through them the Church is made present
in all the various sections of the world
as a sign of hope,
as a source from which hope comes.

Chapter 1

THE VINE AND THE BRANCHES

Dignity of the Lay Faithful

THE MYSTERY OF THE VINE

8 Scripture uses the image of the vine
in a number of ways.
In one case the vine symbolises
the mystery of the People of God.
This stresses that the laity are far more
than mere workers in the vineyard;
they are part of it.

The Old Testament
called Israel God's vine,
his own work, his heart's joy;
and Jesus uses the same symbol to describe
different aspects of the Kingdom of God.
In St. John's Gospel we are led to discover
the mystery of the vine.
It symbolises not only God's people
but Jesus himself.
He is the 'true vine', we are the branches
grafted on to him
and drawing life from him.

Vatican II turns to this same image
describing the Church itself as the vine.
The Church is mystery,
something beyond understanding.
It is mystery because
the life of the Trinity
is freely offered to all the baptised,
who are called to relive
the very oneness and unity of God
and to communicate it to others.

Jesus said
"You will know that I am in my Father
and you in me, and I in you."
Only from inside this mystery
of union or communion,
is it possible to describe the laity's role
in the Church and in the world.

WHO ARE THE LAY FAITHFUL?

9 Previous definitions of the lay faithful
have been largely negative:
'they are not this, not that'.
Looking for something more positive
the Synod studied the words of Vatican II.
Basically the Council declared
that the laity
belong fully to the Church and its mystery.
Further, their vocation
is to build God's kingdom
in all the secular concerns and occupations
of the world around them.
It is Baptism
that unites the faithful with Christ,
that makes them part of God's People,
that lets them share in Christ's role
of prophet, priest and king.

As Pius XII once said,
'the faithful should be aware
not only of belonging to the Church
but of being in the Church'.

To return to the image of the vine,
the laity and all the other members
are branches grafted on to Christ,
drawing life and fruitfulness from him.

It is incorporation into Christ
through Baptism and faith
that makes someone a Christian

in the mystery of the Church,
and this is the basis of all the vocations
and actions of the laity.
In Christ who rose from the dead
the baptised are brought to new life
and become a new creation.

BAPTISM A 'NEW' CHRISTIAN LIFE

10 In attempting to describe the lay faithful
three things must be considered:
that Baptism gives them new life in Christ,
unites them to Christ and to the Church,
and makes them dwellings of God's Spirit.

Children in the Son

11 Baptism is a rebirth, a new life.
As St. Peter said,
'We have been born anew to a living hope
through the resurrection
of Jesus Christ from the dead.' (1 Peter 1:3-4)
With Baptism we become children of God
in his only son Jesus Christ.
This is effected by the Holy Spirit.
'For by one Spirit we are all baptised
into one body.' (1 Cor.12:13)

One Body in Christ

12 The baptised are inseparably linked together
as members of Christ
and members of the Church.
Baptism brings a mystical and real
incorporation into Christ's body.
Through Baptism Jesus unites us
to his death and resurrection,
so that 'We, though many,
are one body in Christ.' (Rom.12:5)
Jesus' own teaching reveals the unity
of his followers and himself
and their unity with each other.

St. Paul echoes these words
and presents that unity as an image
of the mystical communion
between Father, Son and Spirit.

Temples of the Spirit
13 St. Peter said that baptised people
are living stones,
part of a spiritual building in which
Christ is the foundation stone.
Vatican II repeats his words
describing the laity as 'a spiritual house'.
The Holy Spirit makes each one
into a spiritual house
which he fills with God's presence.

Every Christian therefore can say
as Jesus said of himself:
'The Spirit of the Lord is upon me
because he has anointed me
to preach good news to the poor.' (Cf Lk 4.18-19
Thus, every baptised person & Is.61. 1-2)
shares the same mission as Jesus.

SHARERS IN CHRIST'S MISSION
14 The living tradition of the Church has
always recognised that the baptised share
in Christ's mission
of prophet, priest and king.
In the wake of Vatican II
Pope John Paul set out
to emphasise this truth.
'He who was born of the Virgin Mary' he said,
'has come to make us into a kingdom of priests'.
Vatican II reminds us
that the mission of Christ -
Priest, Prophet-Teacher and King -
continues in the Church
and is shared by the whole People of God.
Pope John Paul urges the laity

to absorb the rich teaching of Vatican II
on their sharing in Christ's mission.
Basically, what it teaches is this:-

The laity share Christ's priestly mission.
Incorporated into him
they share in his sacrifice on the Cross
when they offer themselves
and their work to God.
All their daily work and prayer,
their family life and leisure,
their hardships and difficulties too,
become sacrifices offered in the Eucharist
with Christ's sacrifice.
Thus, by their daily life and actions
the laity consecrate the world itself to God.

The laity share Christ's mission
as Prophet-Teacher.
This gives them the capacity
to believe the Gospel
and the responsibility
to proclaim it with courage.
They come to appreciate the Church's faith
that cannot err in matters of belief.
They are called to allow the Gospel's power
to shine out in their everyday lives.
Despite all contemporary contradictions
they must proclaim their hope
of future glory.

The laity share Christ's kingly mission
and he calls them to spread that kingdom.
How do they show this kingship?
Chiefly by their efforts to overcome
the kingdom of evil within themselves.
Then by their service of Christ who is present
in all his sisters and brothers,
they are called to restore to the created world
all its original value.

Doing this they share the power of Christ
who subjects all creation and himself
to the Father so that God
may be everything to everyone. (Cf 1 Cor 15:28)

This sharing in Christ's threefold mission
is begun in Baptism,
developed in Confirmation
and realised in the Eucharist.
It is given to each one individually
because each individually
is one of the many
who form the one Body of Christ.
This sharing
which springs from Church communion
must be lived in communion
and for the deepening of that communion.

SECULAR CHARACTER OF THE LAITY

15 Because of their common dignity
derived from Baptism
all the laity,
all the Church's ordained ministers,
and all the women and men religious,
share responsibility
for the Church's mission.
However, the laity
have a particular responsibility
for as Vatican II said of them:
'their specific character is their secularity'.

The Church exists in the world
even though it does not belong to the world.
It is sent to continue Christ's work
which concerns the saving of humanity
and the renewal of this whole world of time.
All the members of the Church
are called to that work
but they do it in their various ways.
So far as the laity are concerned,

the place where God calls them to work
is in the world around them,
in their ordinary life and work,
and in their relationships.
Their world is not
just an outward framework
but an internal reality
which will find its full meaning in Christ.

So the world becomes the place and the means
whereby the laity fulfil their vocation.
They are called to sanctify the world
by being within it, like salt, like leaven,
and in the way they live
to show Christ to others.

With this in mind,
the Synod insisted
that the word 'secular' must be understood
in the light of God's action.
He has given the world
into the care of women and men
so they can share the work of creation,
can free the created world from its bondage,
find their holiness in marriage or celibacy
and in all the various activities of society.

The Gospel images of salt, light, leaven
have special relevance for the lay faithful.
They are images of deep involvement
and full participation
in the life of the planet,
of the world and of the human community.

CALLED TO HOLINESS

16 The primary vocation of the laity
is to become holy people.
This is true of every member of the Church
without exception.
This vocation is an absolute essential,

springing from the mystery of the Church.
The Church is the vine,
living with Christ's life;
the Church is the Mystical Body
with Christ as its Head;
the Church is the Bride of Christ
who sacrificed himself to make it holy.

The Synod insists that in these days
holiness is even more essential:
'Today we have the greatest need of saints
and we must beg God to raise them up.'
Saints have always been the source of renewal
in difficult times in the Church's history.

The Holy Spirit inspires
each one of the baptised
to follow Jesus -
in listening to the Word of God;
in taking part in liturgy and sacraments;
in personal prayer;
in life in family or community;
in hungering for justice
and in the practice of love and service.

Holiness in the World

17 Lay holiness expresses itself
in involvement in the secular world,
and such a vocation is inseparable
from the new life given by Baptism.
At the same time
this vocation to holiness
is linked with mission
and with responsibility in the Church
and in the world.
The laity's fundamental contribution
to building the Church is their holiness.
The eyes of faith see marvellous things today -
countless lay people, women and men,
engaged in all sorts of work and activities.

They are mostly quite unknown and unnoticed,
tireless labourers in the vineyard,
who go on steadily, through God's grace.
These are the people,
at once humble and great,
who are building God's Kingdom in our time.

During the Synod
a number of lay women and men
were officially canonised
or declared blessed.
At the present time
the whole Church, especially the laity,
can find new models of holiness
lived in the everyday circumstances of life.
The Synod suggests that particular Churches,
that is diocesan Churches,
could well recognise
the examples of lay people
who have lived holy lives
in the secular world,
in marriage and in family life,
and consider proposing them too
for sainthood.

In the light of all these reflections
the words of St. Leo the Great
have meaning:
'Acknowledge, O Christian, your dignity'.

Chapter 2

BRANCHES OF A SINGLE VINE

Participation of the Laity

MYSTERY OF CHURCH COMMUNION

18 Jesus said 'I am the true vine
and my Father is the vine-dresser ...
Abide in me and I in you'. (Cf Jn 15:1,4)
These words show the mystery of communion
that unites Christ and his disciples.
This communion, this oneness,
derives from the oneness of the Trinity,
of Father, Son and Spirit.
Jesus went on to pray that all may be one,
'Even as you, Father, are in me
and I in you'. (Cf Jn 17:21)
Oneness like this, communion like this,
is at the very heart
of the mystery of the Church.

Vatican II and Church Communion

19 A great deal was done by Vatican II
to bring about a clearer understanding
of the Church as communion
and how this applies to life.
What does the word 'communion' say to us?
Basically, it speaks of our union with God
brought about by Jesus in the Spirit.
Opportunities for such communion
are present in the Scriptures
and the Sacraments.
Baptism opens the door to communion,
while the Eucharist is a sign of it
and actually brings it about.

Paul VI spoke of this unity,
calling it the Communion of Saints.
And that is what the Church truly is.
Vatican II pointed to biblical images
which show the Church as a communion -
the sheepfold, the flock, the Holy City,
the vine, the spiritual house
and, above all, the Mystical Body.
In its turn,
the Council suggested a new/old image:
the People of God.
Vatican II described the Church
as a kind of sacrament,
a sign and a means of intimate union with God,
a sign of the unity of the human race,

Therefore it is quite inadequate
to interpret communion in the Church
merely as some sort of sociological reality.
The Church as communion
is the 'new' People, the messianic people
with the dignity and freedom
of God's children,
united through the constant presence
of the Spirit whom they have all received.

An Organic Community

20 Communion in the Church
resembles the unity
of a living functioning body,
It has diversity
and the parts all complement each other.
It has varieties of vocations and ministries,
responsibilities and charisms.
As Vatican II said, recalling St. Paul:
'Just as all the members of the human body
form one body
so do the faithful in Christ.' (Cf 1 Cor.12:1
In the building up of his body
there are many different members

and functions,
yet there is only one Spirit
who gives many varied gifts
to help both the Church and the world.
First among the gifts
is the grace
given by the Holy Spirit
to the apostles,
bringing other people's gifts
under their authority.
Further, the Spirit gives the Body unity
and thus produces love among its members.
So if one member suffers, all suffer;
if one is honoured, all rejoice.
As Vatican II plainly says,
the Holy Spirit is always at the heart
of the Church's unity and diversity,
dwelling in the believers, praying in them,
witnessing that they are God's children.
Not only does he give the Church these gifts,
he is constantly renewing them.
Thus he leads the Church
to oneness with Christ
who is its Bridegroom.

Members of the lay faithful
have to live in fellowship
with all the others,
all committed to making fruitful
the treasure they have been given.
The value of people
does not depend on their gifts,
but on their capacity to serve others.

MINISTRIES AND CHARISMS

21 All gifts and charisms
come from the Holy Spirit.
They are a sharing in Christ's mission.
St. Paul says that God gifted some people
to be apostles,

some prophets or evangelists,
some preachers or teachers.
Whatever the gifts, they are given
to equip the Church for its ministry.

Ordained Ministries

22 In a primary position in the Church
is the ordained ministry,
the one conferred by the Sacrament of Orders.
Jesus chose his apostles
to form and rule his people.
Since then, he has given the same mission
to the bishops who succeed them.
Theirs is a true ministry of service.
Pastors receive from Christ
the authority and power
to serve the Church,
acting in the person of Christ
and, through the Gospel and the Sacraments,
to gather it together.

These ministries, given for the whole Church,
express and bring about
a sharing in Christ's priesthood
that is essentially different
from the laity's sharing.
Yet the ministerial priesthood
is fundamentally directed
to the priesthood of all the faithful.
Pastors then must recognise
that their ministry is meant first of all
for the service of the whole People of God.
In their turn the laity must recognise
that they need this ministry
in order to share in the Church's mission.

Lay Ministries

23 Because the laity share in Christ's mission,
bishops must promote lay ministries
which spring from Baptism and Confirmation

and, for many people, from Matrimony as well.

When necessary and expedient
the clergy can entrust to the laity
various roles and offices
which they normally carry out themselves.
Canon Law lists some of these roles -
to read during the Liturgy of the Word,
to baptise and distribute communion,
to preside over liturgical prayers.
Carrying out these roles
does not turn lay people into clergy.
The clergy become such
through their ordination.

The Synod is grateful for contributions
in this field
made by lay women and men
and for their availability
in situations of necessity.

Today, the lay faithful themselves
are more aware of their part
in the liturgy and its preparation
and are ever more ready to take it.
After all, since the liturgy
is an act of the whole people,
it is natural that the laity
should take on roles
not specifically belonging to the clergy.
At the same time
the Synod found cause for criticism.
Some felt that the word 'ministry'
was used too freely;
that people sometimes confused the common priesthoo
with the priesthood of the clergy;
that Church laws and customs were ignored;
that arbitrary decisions were made
about the laity supplying
for some of the roles
that normally belong to the clergy.

Some found a tendency
to turn lay people into pseudo-clerics
thus creating two parallel structures.

In the light of this situation,
the difference between the two priesthoods
should be made clearer,
as well as the unity
of the Church's mission
in which all share.
When they entrust various roles to the laity,
clergy must act wisely,
showing clearly those ministries and roles
which are based on Baptism,
as well as not abusing the permission
for the laity to supply for them
where there is really no need
or where better planning could avoid it.

Whatever the laity do in the liturgical
or pastoral field
it should be in line
with their specific vocation.
This is a lay vocation
and therefore it differs from the vocation
of the ordained ministers.
Pope Paul VI has written extensively
about the lay vocation
of being present in every area
of today's world;
and this world, he says,
also includes realities like suffering
and human love.
The more lay people are involved
in these realities
the more they will build God's kingdom.

The Synod considered the ministries
of lector and acolyte
which Paul VI had opened up

to the laity, though to men only.
They wanted this to be reconsidered
in the light of current Church practice.
As a result, a commission has been set up
arising from the current increase of ministries
now entrusted to the laity.

Charisms

24 The Holy Spirit enriches the Church
with gifts called charisms.
These take many forms.
The New Testament lists some of them -
healing, working miracles,
prophesying, speaking in tongues.
Whether these gifts
are simple or extraordinary
they are meant for the needs
of the Church and of the world.

There is no lack of charisms today
among the laity, both women and men.
Such gifts are gifts
for the whole Body of Christ
provided they truly come from the Spirit.

As the Synod pointed out,
it is not always easy
to recognise the work of the Spirit.
So every charism needs to be tested.

This is why people with such gifts
need to keep in touch with their pastors
who must judge if these gifts are genuine.

LAY PARTICIPATION IN THE CHURCH'S LIFE

25 Lay participation is expressed
first and foremost
in the life and mission
of the local or particular Church,
the diocese.

Particular Churches and the Universal Church

If they are going to be true participators,
the laity must have a clear picture
of the universal Church
and the particular Church
of their own diocese.
Their particular Church is not a fragment
of the universal Church
nor is the latter the simple sum
of all the particular Churches everywhere.
They are all united
by a real, essential bond.
It is in and through particular Churches,
as Vatican II says, that
the one Catholic Church comes into being.

Lay people should develop
a feeling for their own diocese,
of which their parish is a cell.
They should be ready
to share diocesan projects
and to widen their efforts beyond it
to national and even international fields.
With today's progress in communication
and increasing mobility of peoples,
no part of the world can remain
a closed little group.

To encourage co-operation and dialogue
the Synod favours Diocesan Pastoral Councils.
Where lay people are part of these Councils,
then resources for consultation,
mutual action and decision making
are tremendously strengthened.

Canon law also envisages the lay faithful
taking part in Diocesan Synods
and in local Councils,
and sees this as resulting
in a great contribution
to the Church's mission.

Conferences of Bishops are asked
to evaluate ways
of developing consultation with the laity
at regional and national levels.

The Parish

26 The Church finds its immediate expression
in the parish.
It may lack resources,
it may be widely scattered,
it may be lost to sight in huge cities.
Still, the parish must be seen as the place
where the Mystery of the Church
is made present.
It is no mere geographical area
but a fellowship, the family of God.

The Church's task is too vast
to be left to the parish
so Canon Law
provides means of collaboration
between parishes in a given area.
It also recommends to the bishop's care
various groups of the faithful,
and non-Christians too
who are not under his ordinary pastoral care.
There are many other
places and associations,
whole areas such as education and culture,
where the Gospel can be spread,
but the parish cannot be
the hub of these efforts.
Paul VI said of the parish
that it is indispensable because it creates
the basic community of Christians,
gathers people together in the liturgy,
teaches Christ's message,
and puts Christian love into practice.

The Synod found that in many parishes

there is need for renewal.
Some of them are too large,
some lack resources or priests,
some have specific problems.
If such parishes
are to be true communities
then local clergy
should adapt the parish structures
as Canon Law allows.
Then they can encourage the laity
to share in pastoral responsibilities.
They should also foster
small basic communities,
so-called 'living' communities
where the faithful can spread God's word
and in communion with their priests
express it in love and service
of one another.

Commitment in the Parish

27 Vatican II said that lay activity
within the Church is so vital
that where it is lacking
the mission of the clergy
cannot be fully effective.

Lay activity takes on special meaning
within the parish.
As Vatican II pointed out,
lay people should get used
to working with priests,
bringing out their own and wider problems
for consideration.
And all these problems should be resolved
through general discussion.
As far as they can,
lay people should join in the activities
sponsored by their parish.

The solving of problems
'through general discussion'

should be made easier
when people have a deeper appreciation
of the Parish Pastoral Councils
on which the Synod insists.

If the parish really is the Church
on the local level
then its life and work
is right in the midst of human society,
bound up with its hopes and dramas.
In some parts of the world
society is being dehumanised,
threatened by disintegration,
and the individual lost and bewildered.
Nevertheless, the human heart still thirsts
for friendship,
for personal relationships.
These can be found in the parish
provided it is truly a home for all,
a place of service for all
or as Pope John XIII used to say
'the village fountain'
where people can quench their thirst.

FORMS OF PARTICIPATION

28 All the members of the Church
make up the People of God,
the Body of Christ.
Being a 'member' does not change the fact
that each member is unique.
Christ's call to go into the vineyard
is meant for the Church as a whole,
but equally for each individual member.
St. Gregory the Great summed up this truth:
'In the Holy Church
all are nourished by each one
and each one is nourished by all'.

Individual Participation

Each member of the Church

has a unique task
which no one else can take on.
This individual apostolate,
flowing from a full Christian life,
is the origin of all apostolic action
and there is no substitute for it.
All lay people without exception
are called to this apostolate
and obliged to engage in it.
In some circumstances
this individual apostolate
may be the only possible one.

The individual apostolate
helps to spread the Gospel
and since lay people share fully
the conditions of life and work
and the difficulties of the people around them,
theirs will be a relevant apostolate.
They will be able to reach people's hearts
and open them to the true meaning of life,
to communion with God and with others.

Group Participation

29 The Church has never lacked
associations of the lay faithful.
Third orders, confraternities, sodalities
all show this, even today.
But recent times have seen the spread
of new types of movements,
groups and communities.

Though these new groups
are often very diverse from one another,
they all have the same purpose:
that of sharing in the Church's mission.

The type of formation given in lay groups
will correspond with differing demands.
Such formation expresses the social nature

of the individual person
and gives more drive to their efforts.
Work done as a member of a group
has more effect
than if done as an individual.
It can lead towards transforming society.
This is true enough today
in our fragmented world
with its many problems.
And in a secularised society
these lay groups can help many people
to stay faithful to the Gospel.

Such groups are justified,
and they are necessary.
As Vatican II said,
referring to the group apostolate:
'They are a sign of communion
and of unity within the Church'.

This sign of unity must be visible
in the groups themselves
and in the context
of the Christian community.

Lay people in the Church
are certainly free to form such groups.
This is not by permission of authority.
Their right to do so springs from Baptism.
It is a question of a freedom
to be recognised and guarded
by Church authorities,
a freedom to be exercised
always and only in Church communion.

Criteria for Lay Groups
30 Certain criteria are necessary
for the discernment
and recognition of lay groups.
These are made in the context

of Church mission and communion
and not in opposition
to the right to associate.

First, the group must see
as absolutely basic
the individual's call to holiness.
Whatever the association or group,
it is meant to be a sort of instrument
that guides its members towards holiness.

Second, the group must be responsible
for professing the whole Catholic faith.
Every association should be a forum
where the faith is not only taught
but proclaimed as well.

Third, the group must show itself
to be in communion with the Pope
and with the local Bishop,
holding the Pope
to be the centre of unity
within the universal Church.

This communion with Pope and Bishop
must show itself in a readiness
to accept their teaching
and pastoral initiatives.
It also calls groups to recognise
the legitimate differences between themselves
and a willingness to work together.

Fourth, the group must commit itself
to the Church's apostolate,
bringing a missionary zeal
to its efforts at re-evangelisation.

Fifth, the group must commit itself
to being a presence in human society,
working there to bring about

more just and loving conditions.

These criteria can be verified
in the actual fruits shown by these groups
in their organisations, life and in their work.
Do they appreciate prayer and contemplation,
liturgical and sacramental life,
the vocation of marriage,
the priesthood and consecrated life?
Are they ready to join in activities
organised at local, national,
international level?
Have they a commitment and capacity
for teaching and forming Christians?
Do they want to be witnessing Christians
in the various settings of social life,
and initiators of works of charity?
Have they a spirit of detachment
that makes them generous to others?
Do they draw people to the Christian life
or bring back the lapsed?

The Bishops in Service to Communion
31 If these new groups and associations
sometimes cause understandable problems
the Bishops cannot then stand silent,
both for the sake of the Church
and of the groups themselves.
But their work of discernment
should include guidance
and most of all encouragement.

The time has come to give
official recognition and approval
to some of these groups.

The Synod has already singled out
various movements of Catholic Action
for approval.

The Pontifical Council for the Laity
is currently listing the associations
already approved by Rome.
It is also co-operating
with the Pontifical Council
for the Union of Christians
to work out the basic conditions
for possible approval of ecumenical groups
where Catholics form the majority.

Everyone, clergy and laity,
must try to promote collaboration,
friendship and respect
among the various lay groups
and associations.
Only thus can God's house be built.

Church communion is a gift,
one to be accepted with responsibility,
like the talent in the Gospel story.

Being responsible for this gift
involves us in trying to overcome
any temptation to division and hostility.
St. Paul says:
'I appeal to you ... that you agree,
that there be no dissensions among you,
but that you are united
in the same mind
and in the same judgment'. (Cf 1 Cor.1:10)

Chapter 3

APPOINTED TO BEAR FRUIT

Co-responsibility of the Laity

MISSION TO COMMUNION

32 Because they are grafted on to the vine
one expects the branches to be fruitful.
Life in Christ and in the Church
demands this fruitfulness.
'Without me you can do nothing.' (Cf Jn 15:5)

Communion and mission are intertwined,
each implying the other.
Communion gives rise to mission
and mission finds fulfilment in communion.
The Church recognises this communion
as a gift meant for every individual
and for humanity as a whole.
The Church is 'a sign and instrument
of the unity of all the human race.'
Its mission is to make
all people everywhere
know and love this 'new' communion
which Christ introduced into the world.

In this mission
Christ gives a great responsibility
to lay people.
As Vatican II plainly said,
the pastors of the Church
know only too well
that the Church's mission
is to be carried out by all the faithful,
not simply by themselves alone.
And they realise the greatness of

the laity's contribution.

PROCLAIMING THE GOSPEL

33 It is by Baptism
and by the Spirit's gifts
that the laity are prepared for their task
of proclaiming the Gospel.
Vatican II has described
some of the tasks they take on
in such fields as the liturgy,
in teaching and catechetics,
through skills in personal relationships,
in administration.

The mission of the Church
is summed up in evangelisation.
As Pope Paul VI said,
it is the Church's deepest identity.
It is through evangelisation
that the Church is built up
into a community of true believers.

Christ's command to preach the Gospel
never loses its force.
Today, the present state of the world,
and of many parts of the Church, too,
make his call even more imperative.
He calls each person by name
and no true follower can hold back.

A Time for Re-evangelisation

34 This is a hard testing time
for some of the countries
where Christianity formerly flourished.
They are being radically changed
through a growing indifference,
through atheism and secularism.
This is particularly true of countries
belonging to the so-called 'First World'.
Here consumerism and affluence,

even if co-existing
with poverty and want,
give rise to a way of living
as though God did not exist.

There are further reasons for such decline.
Sometimes the Christian faith
becomes no more than a formality,
the survival of external rituals,
with little to contribute
to significant moments of human life,
and no answers to human dilemmas.
When this happens,
people are left open to delusion
and blinded to spiritual realities.

In other parts of the world,
many traditions of piety remain
as well as popular forms of Christianity;
but these, too, risk destruction
under the weight of many pressures,
including secularism
and the spread of religious sects.
Only re-evangelisation
can bring life back
into these traditions,
making them a force for freedom.

It is undeniable
that the Christian fabric of society
must be mended all over the world.
But before this can be done,
the fabric of the Church community itself
in these countries
needs to be re-made.

This is the time
when the laity have to bear witness
that the only valid response
to human hopes and problems

is the Christian faith.
They can give such witness if they learn
how to integrate the Gospel teaching
with the way they live their lives.

Pope John Paul urges everyone
to open the door to Christ,
to let him enter, with his power,
within the boundaries of states,
into all the fields of culture,
into political and economic systems.
He urges people not to fear to do this.
Only Christ knows what is in people.
Let him speak to their doubts
and uncertainties.
He has the words of eternal life.
To open the door to Christ,
to accept him into humanity itself
poses no threat to anyone.
It is the only path
on which it is possible to arrive
at the fullness of truth
and the dignity of the individual.

The Church owes it to humanity
to proclaim the simple, powerful truth
that God loves every human being,
that Christ came on earth
for every one of them
as the Way, the Truth and the Life.

Re-evangelisation is directed towards
individual people and to whole groups.
Its aim is to create Church communities
mature enough to radiate the faith,
showing that it is a true encounter,
a communion with Christ,
a life lived in love and service.

The laity have their part
in forming these communities,

not only through their own Christian lives
but through an apostolic zeal
towards people who still have no belief
or who have given up their faith.

One contribution
which the laity can make
is systematic work in catechesis.
The Synod pays tribute
to what catechists are doing today
and its great importance
in giving new life
to Church communities.
It goes without saying
that the primary catechists of children
are their parents.
At the same time, we should all realise
that every baptised person has a right
to be instructed and supported
in their Christian faith and life.

Go Out into the World

35 In addition to re-evangelising,
the Church must continue its mission
of bringing Christ's Gospel
to the millions who do not know it.

Lay missionary work is conspicuous today
when it is ever more necessary.
Many lay missionaries,
including married couples,
are ready to leave their own country
and to work for a time in mission territory.

The need for missionary work
is so urgent today
that it calls for truly consolidated efforts
by the entire Church,
individuals and communities.
The particular Churches have to mirror

the universal Church,
so this call to missionise
is addressed to them as well.

The Church today needs
to take giant strides in the tasks
of evangelisation and mission.
The so-called 'younger' Churches
need the strength of the older Churches,
and the latter need the witness, the enterprise
and the vigour of the younger.

In the setting up of new Churches,
a vital element is the formation
not only of a local clergy
but also of a responsible, mature laity.
This is the experience
of the 'young' Churches.

All over the world today
Christians live among people
who believe in other faiths.
All Christians, especially the laity
living among them,
should be a relevant sign
of Christ and the Church.
The laity can help with
dialogue between different religions.
This has great importance
because it leads to mutual respect,
diminishes prejudice
and promotes unity and friendship.

The first need for the evangelisation
of the world
is people who will undertake to do it.
Everyone, from the Christian family onwards,
should feel responsible
for fostering missionary vocations,
whether they come from the clergy,
the religious or the laity.

Every effort must be made in this regard,
but prayer for such vocations
should never be neglected.

LIVING THE GOSPEL: SERVING OTHERS

36 The Church is simultaneously
an evangelising community
and a community that is evangelised.
This makes it the servant of all.
The Church is devoted to the Kingdom of God.
The Church on earth is its beginning.
This Kingdom brings freedom
and salvation to all peoples.
Remembering this,
the Church lives and walks
intimately bound in a real sense
to their history.

The Church awakens one person to another,
opening up to each one
truths about existence
and the meaning of life.
The Church is called to serve everyone
because Christ has united himself
in some fashion to every person.

The individual person then
is the primary path the Church must travel,
the way traced out by Christ himself.

Vatican II stressed this truth,
saying that the Church
in working for the salvation of humanity
not only communicates God's life to all
but casts the reflection of that life
throughout the world.
It does this by restoring human dignity,
strengthening the bonds of society,
by giving a deeper significance
to people's everyday activities.

The Church therefore believes that
both through its individual members
and through the whole community
it can help towards making life on earth
more genuinely human.

In this work for humanity
and the secular world
the laity have a special role.
This is where they are called to work.

Promoting Human Dignity
37 An essential service
which the Church can do
for the whole human family
is to rediscover
and make others rediscover
the dignity of every person.

In the whole of creation
only a woman or a man is a 'person',
a conscious and free human being.
The most precious possession
of any individual
is human dignity.
A person has more value
than anything else in the created world.
It is not from 'what they have'
that this value springs
but from 'what they are'.

Human beings are created by God,
redeemed by Christ,
made temples for the Spirit,
and called to a life of oneness with God.
In the light of this,
every violation of human dignity
cries out to God for vengeance.

Because they have this dignity

people may never be treated
as things, mere objects to be used.

Human dignity is the basis
of human equality.
Therefore no discrimination of any sort
is acceptable.
It is an intolerable injustice,
not only because of the tensions it causes,
but because it dishonours the dignity
of the victim
and still more of the perpetrator.
Personal dignity is also the basis
of solidarity among all peoples.
Dialogue and communion are rooted ultimately
in what people 'are'
rather than in what they 'have'.

The individual person can never be reduced
to the anonymity that comes
from certain structures and systems.
The individual is not just a number,
an impersonal link in a chain,
a cog in some machine.
The greatest assertion that was ever made
about the value of every human being
was made by Christ when he became man.

The Right to Life

38 The acknowledgment of human dignity
demands respect for human rights,
and their defence and protection.
These rights are universal and inherent.
They cannot be changed or eliminated
by any authority whatever,
because these rights are from God.

The most basic human right
is the right to life.
Many voices are justifiably raised

on behalf of the rights to work,
to a home, to health, to a family.
But these will lead nowhere
unless the basic right to life
is inexorably defended.

The Church has never given way
in the face of violations
of the right to life.
Vatican II has spelled out
some of these violations:
murder, genocide, abortion,
mutilation and torture,
sub-human living conditions,
slavery and prostitution.
Acts like this poison society.
They are a dishonour to the Creator.

Though everyone is called
to defend the right to life
some lay people have special responsibility:
for example, parents and teachers,
health workers,
and people with political power.

One aspect of the Church's mission
is to accept every human being,
especially the sick and the weak,
with love and generosity.
The Church sees all life
as a gift from God.
In the darkness of today's world
of pessimism and selfishness
the Church stands for life;
in the face of the world's 'No'
it gives a living 'Yes'.

Biological and medical science
have developed enormously.
So has the power of technology.
This provides new possibilities

on the very frontiers of human life,
and such possibilities
imply new responsibilities.
In fact, today humanity
can exercise control
over human life at its beginnings
and in its first stages of development.
In the face of such great strides
the moral conscience of humanity
cannot remain indifferent.

From those engaged in scientific research
a true wisdom is called for,
a wisdom that shows itself
in intelligence and life,
in a respect for the dignity of the person
from the first moments of life's existence.
Science and technology
have legitimate ways
of defending life or curing disease
in its beginnings,
but they should refuse,
even for the dignity of research itself,
to perform operations that result
in the falsification
of the genetic inheritance of the individual
or of human generative power.

Lay people with responsibility
in the medical, social,
legislative or economic fields
must courageously take on the challenge
posed by new problems in bio-ethics.
The Synod said that Christians
should exercise their responsibilities
as the masters of science and technology,
and not become their slaves.

Everyone should remain vigilant
before the increasing power of technology.
It has a tendency to manipulate

not only the biological essence of humanity
but the very content
of people's consciences as well.

Basic Religious Freedom

39 There is a religious dimension
to every human being
and this must be respected.
'It is in God that we live and move
and have our being.' (Cf Acts 17:28
Not everyone believes this
but those who do believe have the right
to be respected for their faith.
Human dignity demands freedom of religion.
It is a point of reference and a measure
of the other basic human rights.

The Synod did not forget the many people,
most of them Christian lay people,
who are deprived of such freedom,
who face persecution and suffering
and sometimes death for their belief.
To witness to the Gospel
amid suffering and martyrdom
is the peak of a Christian life
and a source of strength to the Church.

The Synod described its gratitude
for the courage of these Christians,
for the tireless witness they give,
for the way they risk everything.

The problem of human rights
has a world dimension today
when groups of people,
indeed entire nations
are being violently deprived of them.
Pope John Paul II
has denounced this unjust situation
in 'Sollicitudo Rei Socialis'

which he wrote in 1988.

Respect for each person demands more
than an individual morality;
it means concern for society.

The very structure of society
demands respect for the individual
because society's whole purpose
is geared to the human person.

Service to the person goes hand-in-hand
with service to society.

The Family

40 There is an inherent social dimension
to every person
which calls the individual
into communion with others.
God has willed that all people everywhere
should form one family
of sisters and brothers.

This means that society and individuals
are interdependent.
What helps one helps the other.
The apostolate of the laity,
which is directed to both,
should be viewed in this light.

The basis of this social dimension
is the married couple and the family.
The family is the primary cell of society,
the place where an individual
is born and grows.
The family needs protection against
the attacks that threaten it,
whether these come from human egoism,
anti-birth campaigns, political schemes,
or from poverty and want.

This situation calls for
enormous, systematic efforts,
and such efforts should be upheld,
not only by cultural aids
but also by the law of the land
and economic help to those in need.

The laity have the duty
to bring the family to a realisation
of its basic role in society
so that it may become more alive
and responsible for proper growth
and proper participation in social life.
All those who are concerned for the family
can find a complete programme of work
in Pope John Paul's 'Familiaris Consortio'
and in the Charter of Rights for the Family.
This was drawn up by the Holy See
at the request of the 1980 Synod of Bishops.
There is increasing need today
to put this programme into decisive action.

Whole civilisations stand or fall
on the human quality of their families.
The Church is absolutely convinced
that the path towards the future
passes through the family.

Charity
41 Service to society is expressed
through charity to one's neighbour
and the whole Church is called to this.
Charity can take many different forms,
the most important being
the spiritual and corporal works of mercy
expressed in contemporary forms.
This will lead to the Christianisation
of the world around them,
the task to which the laity are called.

It is through charity to others

that the laity share in Christ's mission.
For he came 'not to be served but to serve'.
Such a service is possible for everyone
and all the time.

Charity to our neighbours,
whether exercised by individuals
or by communities or groups,
will always be needed.
Nothing can replace it,
not even the initiatives and societies
set up to help the needs
of whole populations of people.
As a matter of fact
such societies can, in the end,
become so impersonal and bureaucratic
that they cease to be effective.

There is a continual increase
in the number of lay volunteers
who undertake all sorts of services.
When their help is truly given
for the good of all,
especially for the needy and forgotten,
then it must be considered
an important expression
of the lay apostolate.

Public Life

42 Charity and justice are inseparable,
and each demands a full acknowledgment
of human rights.
The Synod has stressed repeatedly
the right and duty of everyone
to take part in public life,
in various fields
and on various levels.
No matter what accusations
may be thrown at those in public life:
for instance, that they are opportunists,

or that they worship power;
still, the laity are never justified
in keeping aloof from it.

Vatican II stood up
for the people involved in public life
and praised their work and dedication.

The work of such people is always directed
to the common good.
By the common good is meant the sum total
of all the conditions of social life
whereby individuals, families and groups
are helped to grow and develop.

Work in public life or in politics
will always be concerned
with the promotion of justice
and with the spirit of service.
To be seen to work for these things
will put those who do so
beyond the range of accusations so often made.
But it is not easy to achieve this.
To do so requires rising above temptations
to disloyalty and dishonesty,
to the misuse of public funds,
to favouritism and illicit ways
of clinging to power at any price.

Vatican II believed it important
to have a right view of the relationship
between the Church
and the political community.
A clear distinction should be made
between the actions
of Christians as citizens
and the actions of Christians
in the name of the Church.
The Church is in no way identified
with any one political community
nor bound to any political system.

The Church is a sign and a safeguard
of the supreme value of the human person.
At the same time, the laity must witness
to all the human and Gospel values
connected with political activities.
These values include freedom and justice,
a simple life-style, unselfishness,
solidarity and a special love for the poor.

If public life is to ensure
the fostering of true human development,
then there must be solidarity.
As Pope John Paul said,
solidarity is not some vague compassion
over people's misfortunes;
'it is a determination to commit oneself
to the common good
because we are all
really responsible for all'.

Today, political solidarity
requires going beyond single nations.
It is concerned with blocks of nations
and with the whole world.
The result of sound political activity
is peace,
the universal longing.
The laity cannot remain inactive
in the face of all that denies peace -
evils such as war,
violence, torture and terrorism.
concentration camps. the arms race,
the nuclear threat.

The laity who serve in peace organisations
at national or international levels
should promote the widest spread
of peace education.
Such education would be directed
to overcoming the evils of
hatred, hostility and egoism,

and thus build up solidarity.
Such solidarity leads both to peace
and to development.

The Synod called on Christians
to reject all forms of violence
and to commit themselves to creating
a just international and social order.

The Individual at the Centre of Socio-economic Life

43 The Church's social doctrine
is based on the principle
that the earth's goods
are meant for everyone,
so that everyone can live
a truly human life.
Private property is meant
to serve this end,
and so is human work.
Work is the most immediate means
by which economic life can be developed.
Vatican II says that

in social and economic life
the dignity of the human person
must be recognised and promoted,
since the individual is the source,
the centre and the purpose
of all economic life.

In the world of economy and work
the laity must be in the forefront
in working out solutions
to the severe problem of unemployment.
They must fight to overcome injustice,
to gain for workers
the respect that is their due,
to build new solidarity between them
to create new forms of entrepreneurship.
And they should take a hard look

at systems of commerce, finance
and the exchange of technology.

To be able to do all this,
the laity will need professional competence,
a true Christian spirit
and plain human honesty.

The question of ecology
becomes even more important today.
Humanity has the God-given task
of 'cultivating the garden' of our planet.
This has to be done
with intelligence and love.
We have to hand on this gift
to future generations
and, if possible,
in a better state than it is today.
God's words 'to dominate' the creation
give humanity no freedom to abuse it.
When it comes to the natural world
we are subject,
not only to biological laws,
but to moral laws as well.
And they cannot be violated
without disastrous consequences.
A true concept of development
cannot ignore the way the planet is used
nor which of its resources are renewable,
nor the consequences
of haphazard industrialisation.
These considerations make us realise
that there is a moral dimension
to development.

Evangelising Culture

44 Service to human society is expressed
in the creation
and transmission of culture.
Vatican II defined culture

as everything that helps
human beings to develop their potential,
that makes their lives more human,
that helps them to express
great spiritual experiences
and the deepest human desires.
Culture then is the common good
of all people,
the means by which they express
their dignity, freedom,
creativity and identity.

When culture ceases to be linked
with the Christian faith
or with true human values,
then the Church's pastoral concern
must be involved.
This is equally true in situations
where science and technology
can give no answers to deep questions
about life and the human condition.
Therefore, the Church calls the laity
to be present
in the privileged places of culture,
in the worlds of education
and scientific research,
in the areas of artistic creativity
and of work in the humanities.

Vatican II said that
the Gospel continually renews
the life and culture of fallen humanity.
In this way
the Church carries out its mission
and makes its contribution
to human and civic culture.
Pope Paul VI said that
the split between the Gospel and culture
was, without doubt,
the drama of our time.
Therefore, every effort must be made

to ensure a full evangelisation of cultures.

Social communication
has the most privileged position of all
in the creation
and transmission of culture.
The world of the mass-media,
constantly developing,
constantly innovating,
exerts a world-wide influence
on the way people think and behave.

Lay people who work professionally
in this field
have to see that the value
of the mass-media is recognised
and that it is sustained
by more adequate resource material,
whether intellectual or pastoral.

The use of the mass-media
by professional communicators
and its reception by the general public
call for an education in criticism,
inspired by a passion for the truth.
It also demands a defence of liberty,
a respect for individual dignity
and a promotion of authentic culture.
This will come about
when every sort of manipulation
and monopoly are firmly rejected.

The laity's responsibility in this field
does not stop with the work of defence.
It also involves
the proclamation of the Gospel
by all the professionals working in radio,
cinema, press, theatre and television.

Chapter 4

WORKERS IN THE LORD'S VINEYARD

Stewards of God's Graces

MANY DIFFERENT VOCATIONS

45 In the story of the vineyard
the owner called people to work for him
at different hours of the day.
This can stand for the way
in which people are called
at various stages in their lives
to make the Church present in society.

Young People

46 In many countries of the world,
half the entire population
is made up of young people.
This proportion holds true
of the Church in these countries.
Young people present a potential
and a challenge to the Church's future.
Vatican II referred to them
as 'the hope of the Church'.

Young people can and should be inspired
to lead in the evangelisation of society
and to share in its renewal.
Youth is a time for self-discovery,
for a choice of life
and for growth.

Young people are naturally drawn
to friendship and solidarity,
to the values of peace,
non-violence and justice.

They respond to ecological causes
and want to care for the earth.
But along with all of this
they are troubled by anxieties,
anguishes and fears of the world,
and by all the temptations of their youth.
To all these fears and hopes
the Church offers one unique response.
It is Jesus Christ and his Gospel

The Church and young people
have so much to share
and to talk about.
Such dialogue will provide
an exchange between different generations
and will be a source of youthfulness
both for the Church and for society.

Children
47 Jesus loved children
and promised them the Kingdom of Heaven.
Even in the stage of childhood
there is scope for building the Church
and humanising society.

As Vatican II often pointed out,
children are vital members of the family,
of 'the Church at home',
and in their own way
they help to sanctify their parents.
This is equally true in a wider sense,
in relation to the local Church
and the universal Church as well.

Older People
48 The Church expects its older members
to carry on their mission.
Biblical imagery loves to show
older people as full of wisdom.
And in this sense today

the gift of older people can be
to witness to tradition
and to teach what the Bible calls
the lessons of life. (Cf Sir 6:34; 8:11-12)

Today, older people are becoming
more and more numerous everywhere.
This brings new apostolic possibilities.
Part of their mission
is a refusal to sink into nostalgia,
to want to live in a past
that will never return,
to refuse responsibilities
because of difficulties inherent in change.
They need to know clearly
that their role in the Church
does not stop with age.
What does change
is the way they fulfil it.

The Church never under-rates
the value of its older members.
Despite all the physical and social problems
which ageing brings,
the Church sees them
at a stage in life
that can be humanly and spiritually fruitful.
In the plan of God,
each one lives a life of constant growth,
from the beginning of existence
to the moment of death.

WOMEN AND MEN

49 Confronted with the discrimination,
the marginalisation,
to which women are subjected
just because they are women,
the Synod insisted
on the urgent need to promote
women's personal dignity

and their equality with men.

If anyone has to work to advance
the dignity of women in Church and society,
it is women themselves
who must see their responsibility.
Great efforts are still needed today
to destroy the vicious mentality
that considers people as things,
a mentality that counts women
as its main victims.
Women's personal dignity
must be openly acknowledged,
because this is the first step towards
their full participation in Church life
and in social and public life.
The Synod urges the Church
to oppose all forms of discrimination
and abuse of women.

Because women now share more fully
in the life of society,
it is important that they share more fully
in the Church's apostolate.
The fact that women
have a specific vocation
has only been gradually realised
since Vatican II.
And this realisation has been inspired
by the Gospel story.

Though women were not called
to the mission of the Twelve Apostles
and the ordained ministry,
they were closely associated with Jesus
all through his ministry,
and in his passion,
his burial and resurrection.

All through the Church's development
there have been women

who exercised decisive roles
and accomplished great things on its behalf.
These may often have been
hidden and quite humble deeds,
but their result was no less decisive
for the Church's growth and holiness.
Today, women should continue
and expand their roles.

In line with what Vatican II had said,
the Synod made this recommendation:
'It is necessary that the Church
recognise all the gifts of women and men
for its life and mission
and put them into practice.'

Femininity and Masculinity:
True Dignity of the Sexes

50 If women are to take their rightful place
in Church and society,
there should be a clarification
of their personal identity in relation to men.
The Synod felt this to be necessary
for resolving questions
about the significance
and dignity of each sex.

In reflecting on this,
the Church sees itself
making a true contribution
towards the advancement of women.
But before this,
it wants to speak in obedience to God
who created the individual to his image,
made them male and female
and intended them to live
according to his plan for them;
a plan which has been imprinted
deep within the very being
of every individual

right from the beginning.
The richness inherent in this plan
came to be shown progressively
through the whole history of salvation
and it was brought to completion
when God became man,
'born of a woman'. (Cf Gal 4:4)

God's plan for women is to be seen
in the context of faith
and in the lives of so many
Christian women today.
The help rendered
by the various human sciences
should not be overlooked
when attempting to clarify
the values that belong
to the essential aspects of woman,
and the ones that evolve in history.
Vatican II pointed out
that beneath all changes
there are some realities
that never change.

The Synod draws attention
to a meditation composed by
Pope John Paul II and called
'The Dignity and Vocation of Woman'.
This could be an incentive
for women and men alike,
particularly those engaged in the fields
of theology and the human sciences,
to make a critical study
aimed at a deeper understanding
of the specific values and gifts
both of femininity and masculinity.
These should be studied
as they are manifested
both in the surroundings of social living
and also in Christian living
and in membership of the Church.

Pope John Paul's meditation
ought to enlighten the Christian response
to ever-recurring questions
as to women's rightful place
in the Church and in society.

It is clear
from Christ's own words and attitude
that no discrimination exists
on the level
of individual relations with him.
Nor does any exist
in the Church's life of grace and holiness.
As Pope John Paul says:
'Both women and men are equally capable
of receiving divine truth
and life in the Holy Spirit.'

Women's Mission in Church and World
51 It is undeniable
that women and men are both called
to share in the Church's apostolate.
And women are called to use
their own particular gifts in this work.

A woman cannot be ordained
so she cannot fulfil the role
of the ministerial priesthood.
The Church sees this practice
as the will of Christ,
who called only men to be his apostles.
This practice can be understood
from the relations
between Christ the Bridegroom
and the Church, his Bride.
All this is concerned only with function
and not with dignity or holiness.

Pope Paul VI said:
'We cannot change what our Lord did,

nor his call to women
but we can recognise and promote
the role of women in evangelisation
and the life of the Christian community.'

It is not enough to theorise
about women's responsibility
in the Church.
Theory has to become practice.
As a sign of this,
the term 'women and men'
has been repeatedly
used in this Exhortation to the Laity.
Furthermore,
the Revised Code of Canon Law
has many provisions
on women's participation
in the Church's life and mission.
These provisions
should be known more widely
and where they are relevant
should be put into practice
with more vigour.

One example is women's participation
on diocesan and parochial pastoral councils,
as well as on Diocesan Synods
and particular Councils.
The Synod believes that women
ought to be associated in the preparation
of pastoral and missionary documents,
and to be recognised
as co-operators in the Church's mission
in the family, in professional work
and in the caring community.

Women should also be encouraged
to work in the more specific fields
of evangelisation and catechesis,
not only in the family but also
in the various educational settings.

While evangelising others,
women have to realise
that they themselves
need to be evangelised.
Then they will be able to distinguish between
what truly fosters their human dignity
and the false values that endanger it
under the guise of 'freedom' and 'progress'.
Such false values are responsible
for the moral degradation of individuals,
of the environment
and of society.

All the problems of today's world
call for the presence
and commitment of women.

Two great tasks are entrusted to women.
The first is to bring its full dignity
to married life and to motherhood.
Today, women have new opportunities
for a deeper understanding,
a richer realisation of these things.
When they make use of these opportunities
they can bring the man,
husband and father,
to play a full part
in responsible parenthood
and in building up the marriage.

Women's second task is to ensure
a moral dimension
to culture and human activities,
to create a culture worthy of the person
and of humanity.

The personal dignity of women,
and their specific vocation,
ought to be respected and promoted
in all aspects
of the life of the community,

from the socio-economic aspect
to the socio-political.
This is equally true in the case
of situations which affect
either the individual or the community,
or when women work
in voluntary or statutory fields.

In a special way, every human being
is entrusted to woman.
Because of this experience,
woman seems to possess
a specific sensitivity
towards the human person
and to its true welfare.
This gives her great scope
and great responsibility today
when the development
of science and technology
is not always inspired by real wisdom
and so runs the risk
of dehumanising human life,
just at the time when life needs
to become more, not less human.

It is through sharing their gifts
in the Church and in society
that women find their path
of personal fulfillment.

Collaboration of Women and Men

52 In the Synod, fears were expressed
that so much stress on the role of women
would result in too little emphasis
on the role of men.
In fact, in many parts of the Church
men are scarce or virtually absent.
Some abdicate their responsibilities
in the Church,
leaving women to fulfil them.

The Synod lists
some of these responsibilities:
the liturgy, education,
the teaching of religion to their own
and other children,
presence at religious gatherings,
sharing in charitable
and missionary initiatives.

From the pastoral point of view
the co-ordinated presence
of women and men is necessary
if the laity are to make
the Church's mission
richer and more complete.

The fundamental reason why women and men
should collaborate is because
this is part of God's original plan.
He willed the human being
to be 'a unity of two'.
He willed women and men to be
the primary community of persons,
the source of all other communities.
At the same time, he willed them
to be a 'sign'
of the interpersonal community of love
which is the life of the Trinity.

For this reason,
the most basic means of ensuring
the presence of women and men
in the Church's mission
is through the tasks and responsibilities
of the married couple and the Christian family.

Here, many forms of life and love
are witnessed and experienced:
married love, parental love,
filial and family love.
The Christian family also builds up

the Kingdom of God
through the everyday realities
that mark out its life:
oneness, faithfulness and fruitfulness.

The Synod stressed the urgent need
for every Christian
to live and proclaim
the message of hope contained in marriage.

THE SICK AND SUFFERING

53 People are called to joy.
All the same they daily experience
every sort of suffering.
The Synod addressed all these people,
the sick, the handicapped,
poor and lonely people,
migrants and prisoners,....
reminding them that the Church
shares their suffering.

In this vast world of human misery,
sickness is the most frequent
and common expression of suffering.
Christ's call to work in his vineyard
is addressed to each and everyone.
The sick, too, are sent forth
as workers in the vineyard
and are called to share
in the growth of God's Kingdom
in a new, more valuable way.
What St. Paul said of himself
may help them
to see the grace
in their actual situation:
'In my flesh I complete what is lacking
in Christ's afflictions
for the sake of his body,
that is the Church.' (Cf Col 1:24)
From a realisation like this,

joy can spring up,
a joy filled with the Holy Spirit.
Such a realisation was expressed
at the Synod by a handicapped person
who spoke these words:
'Christians who suffer are called by God
not only to unite their suffering
to Christ's,
but also to receive in themselves now,
and to transmit to others,
the power of renewal
and the joy of the risen Christ.'

From century to century,
the Christian community
has shown Christ's love
by the way it has cared for
vast numbers of sick and suffering people.
In doing this, it has re-enacted
the Gospel story of the Good Samaritan.
The Church has done this
through the tireless dedication
of doctors, scientists, nurses, volunteers,
and all those engaged
in every form of health care.
Today, increasing numbers
of lay women and men
are working in hospitals
and health-care institutions.
All these people are called to be
the living sign of Christ and his Church
in the care and love they manifest.

Renewed Pastoral Action

54 This precious heritage
of caring for the sick and suffering
must be enriched
through new pastoral initiatives.

One aim of these initiatives

is to create an attitude which regards
sick and handicapped people
not only as people to be loved and served
but as responsible partners
in the Church's mission.
Within a society that has lost
a sense of human suffering,
the Church has to make the news resound
that suffering can have
a positive meaning
for the individual person
and, indeed for society as well.
This is because each person
is called to share
in Christ's redemptive suffering
and the joy of resurrection.

Words like this become believable
when they are seen to be more than words,
when they flower in the way in which
a person cares for the sick and suffering,
or when they flower in the personal lives
of the sick themselves.

In his letter 'Salvifici Doloris',
Pope John Paul II called on
all suffering believers,
especially those who suffer
for Christ's sake,
to gather in spirit on Calvary
and there to offer their suffering
to bring about Christ's prayer for unity.
He said:
'Beside Mary who stood by the cross,
we stand by all the crosses
of contemporary women and men,
asking them in their weakness to support us,
to be a source of strength
for the Church and for the world.'

States of Life and Vocations

55 All the People of God,
clergy, religious or lay people,
work in the one vineyard of God;
each with particular gifts and ministries,
different yet complementary.

All are living members of Christ's Body,
built up through the power of the Spirit.
Being a Christian does not arise
simply from the life
of grace and holiness:
it also arises from the state of life
that is specific to clergy,
to laity and to women and men religious.

In the communion of the Church,
these states all share
the same basic meaning.
Each is a way of living out
the common Christian dignity
and the common call to holiness.
Each state of life
has its own distinguishing features,
yet at the same time
each one is seen
in relation to the others
and placed at each other's service.

The distinguishing feature
of the lay state
is its secularity.
It witnesses to clergy and religious
the significance of earthly realities
in God's plan.
In its turn,
the ministerial priesthood
stands for the permanent guarantee
of Christ's sacramental presence.
The distinguishing feature

of the religious state
is its thrust towards the Kingdom of God
which in some way it anticipates
and experiences even now
through the vows of poverty,
chastity and obedience.

All these states of life,
both individually and collectively,
stand at the service of the Church.

In this diversity of states of life
and of vocations,
the Church manifests and experiences
the richness of the mystery of Christ.
Some of the early Fathers
liked to refer to the Church as a meadow
filled with a wonderful variety of flowers.

Vocations in the Lay State
56 This rich variety is found
even within the different states of life.
Within the lay state
there are different apostolic paths.
Within the lay state
are secular institutes
with their great diversity.
In secular institutes lay people
and clergy, too, find the opportunity
of professing the evangelical counsels.
Yet in doing this
they remain clergy or lay people;
they do not change their state of life.

St. Francis de Sales,
who did much to promote lay spirituality,
has spoken of Christian people
as living plants of the Church.
As God called earth's plants to bear fruit,
so he calls these living plants

to do the same,
according to their various vocations
and characters.

Vatican II said much the same:
Lay spirituality takes its character
from the circumstances of one's life,
whether this is in marriage, celibacy,
family life or widowhood,
and from one's professional
and social activities.

All this can be said
with even more relevance
about the vast number of ways
in which all the members of the Church
are employed in Christ's vineyard.
Here, each one is called by his or her name.
Each one is asked
to make a special contribution
to the coming of Christ's Kingdom
and no talent is too small to be used.

Chapter 5

BEARING FRUIT

Formation of the Laity

GROWING TO MATURITY

57 The image of the vine and its branches
shows another aspect of lay mission:
the call to grow to maturity.

God calls everybody to bear fruit,
to grow and develop,
and they may not postpone their response
nor deny their responsibility.

Between God offering his gifts,
and the person called to respond,
comes the possibility and need
for on-going lay formation.
The Synod has plainly said
that a diocese must put
the formation of the laity
among its priorities.

The efforts of the whole diocese,
clergy, religious and laity,
should be directed to this end.

TO LIVE ONE'S VOCATION

58 The formation of the laity should
bring them an ever clearer discovery
of their mission,
and a readiness to fulfil it.
At the same time, it should help them
to recognise their own human dignity.

God has loved us from eternity
as unique individuals,
but it is only as our lives unfold
that his plans for us are revealed.
This is something that happens day by day.

To discover his will for us
means listening to Christ
and the Church,
praying with fervour,
accepting spiritual guidance,
discerning the gifts he has given us
in the situations of our lives.

Special decisive times occur
in each one's life
for discerning God's will.
Among these times
are adolescence and young adulthood.

It is not enough to know
what God wants from each of us
in our life situations.
We also have to do what he wants.
This requires a capacity to act,
a capacity that must be developed.
This capacity is not beyond us.
As St. Leo the Great said:
'The One who confers the dignity
will give the strength.'

To grow in the knowledge
of all that our faith gives us,
to live it out more fully -
this is the task awaiting all Christians
at every moment of their lives.

INTEGRATED FORMATION
FOR AN INTEGRATED LIFE

59 Lay formation must take into account

that lay people are members of the Church
and also citizens of human society.

They do not live two parallel lives:
one spiritual life with its own demands,
one secular life with the demands
of home, work, and the world around them.
In God's plan,
every area of life without exception
is meant to reveal Christ's love.
Every activity and situation,
every responsibility, offers occasions
for glorifying God and serving others.

Vatican II spelled out the dangers
of putting life into two compartments,
of separating faith from living
and the Gospel from human culture.
'The split between the faith
which many profess
and their daily lives
deserves to be counted among
the more serious errors of our age.'

Aspects of Formation

60 Importance should be given
to a person's spiritual formation.
Vatican II has described
how the life of union with Christ
is strengthened by spiritual helps
readily available,
such helps, for example, as the liturgy.

Today, the laity in general
need a doctrinal formation,
not simply to give them
a better knowledge of the faith,
but to enable them
'to give a reason for their hoping',
in spite of the grave problems

that exist everywhere in the world.
A systematic approach to catechesis,
geared to age and life situations,
is absolutely essential.
So is a more definite
Christian promotion of culture,
in response to the current questions
concerning the individual and society.

Lay people who have responsibilities
in various fields of public life
need formation.
They need a better understanding
of the Church's social teaching.
It is not enough simply to exhort people
to engage in public life.
The Synod stressed that
they must be offered a proper formation
of a social conscience,
especially in the Church's social teaching,
which contains principles of reflection,
criteria for judging,
and practical directives.

In a truly integrated formation
human values will be cultivated
and held in great respect.
Vatican II has described
how the laity should esteem
professional skill,
family and civic spirit,
and all the good human qualities
like honesty, sincerity, courtesy,
justice and moral courage.
Where these are lacking
there is no true Christian life.
In making their lives an organic whole
the laity are to be guided by the Spirit.

CO-OPERATORS WITH GOD THE TEACHER

61 Who is responsible
for providing the laity
with an integrated formation?
Human education is inseparable
from the work of fathers and mothers.
Christian formation is inseparable
from God the Father
who is the first and great Teacher
of his people.

God's work of forming his people
is fulfilled in Christ the teacher
and is made effective through the Spirit.
The Church is called to participate
in this formation
through a sharing of its life,
through its actions,
and various pronouncements.
Thus, the laity are formed
within the Church
and by the Church,
with all the members cooperating.

The Church is a teacher
where the Pope takes the primary role
in forming the laity.
His ministry is to strengthen
his sisters and brothers in the faith,
and to instruct believers
about their vocation
and their mission in the Church.
The laity should be ready to listen
to his words
and to the words that come from
the Holy See's various departments.

Within the particular Churches or dioceses,
the bishop has a responsibility
towards the laity,
providing guidance and animation

through preaching the Word,
through celebrating the Eucharist
and the Sacraments.

Within the diocese,
the parish is responsible
for a more immediate formation,
for the parish can more easily reach
individual people and groups.
It should instruct the parishioners
in Scripture,
in the liturgy and prayer,
and in the practice of a life of charity.

Within a parish, especially a huge parish,
small church communities can help
in the formation of the laity.
They provide an experience
of Church communion, of Church mission.
The Synod has also advocated
a post-baptismal catechesis
based on the Rite
of Christian Initiation of Adults.
From this, people can come to see
all the riches and responsibilities
which their Baptism has given them.

Whether in diocese or parish,
various members of the Church
can help in each other's formation.
Priests and religious
should be included in this.
The Synod also wants priests and ordinands
to be trained to help with lay formation.
Similarly, the laity themselves
can and should help priests and religious
on their spiritual journey.

Other Places for Formation
62 The family is the domestic Church,

the Church at home,
the place where children receive
formation for Christian living.
As parents come to understand
how their 'domestic church'
shares in the life and mission
of the whole Church,
so their children will come to feel
'a sense of the Church'
and will want to work for it.

Universities and Catholic schools,
and centres of spiritual renewal
are all places of formation.
While it is still necessary for parents
to be involved in school life,
this by itself is not enough today.
Parents have to be formed to realise
that bringing up their children
is part of their own mission
in the Church.
Parents, together with teachers,
clergy and religious,
and representatives of young people,
all make up 'a communion of formation'.
To make sure that the school
can really provide formation,
the laity should insist
on a genuine freedom in education,
for everyone and from everyone.
And, if need be,
they should resort to civil legislation
to achieve this.

The Synod encourages women and men
who are involved in education.
It stresses the importance
of their being true witnesses
to the Gospel.
Their witness is given
by the way they live,

by their professional competence,
their Christian-based teaching
which always respects the autonomy
of their various sciences and disciplines.
These women and men can help others
to understand the connection
between faith and science,
between the Gospel and human culture.

Groups, movements and associations,
all have their place in lay formation,
each with its particular method,
each offering a shared experience
in the apostolic life

RECIPROCAL FORMATION

63 Formation is not just for an elite.
It is intended for everybody,
and everyone has a right to it.
This will involve a great extension
and will call for the formation of people
whose task will be to form others.

In Christian formation
the greatest attention must be given
to indigenous culture.
When it seems necessary,
the Church should also be aware
of the cultures
of minority ethnic groups
and where it is necessary
to protect them.

One cannot offer other people
a genuine formation
unless they have taken on
a personal responsibility
for it themselves.

The more we are formed ourselves

and the more we feel the need to deepen it,
the better we can form other people.

Formation must make use of every sort
of scientific aid and method.
Still, it is openness to the action of God
that makes it truly effective.

AN APPEAL AND A PRAYER

64 Pope John Paul II
appeals to everyone in the Church
to keep in their hearts
what membership of the Church means.

Through Baptism they have been given
an extraordinary dignity.
They are children loved by the Father,
members of Christ's body,
temples of the Spirit.

The new life through Baptism
is the basis
for all sharing in Christ's mission.
For the laity, this sharing is expressed
through the secularity
which is their characteristic feature.

A real sense of Church communion
will bear its fruit
in a variety of vocations,
charisms, ministries and works,
and in the collaboration
of varying groups.

The whole Church
now stands at the door
of the Third Millennium.
This makes it feel ever more strongly
its responsibility to preach the Gospel.
A great challenge faces the Church,

namely, to re-evangelise the world.

The Synod entrusts this work
to the prayers of Mary Mother of Christ,
and Pope John Paul does likewise,
praying to her in these words:

O Virgin full of courage,
may your spiritual strength
and trust in God inspire us,
so that we may know
how to overcome all the obstacles
that we encounter
in accomplishing our mission.
Teach us to treat the affairs
of the world
with a real sense
of Christian responsibility
and a joyful hope
of the coming of God's Kingdom, and
of a 'new heaven and a new earth'.

O Virgin Mother,
guide and sustain us
so that we may always live
as true sons and daughters
of the Church of your Son.
Enable us to do our part
in helping to establish on earth
the civilization of truth and love,
as God wills it,
for his glory. Amen

SUGGESTED DISCUSSION THEMES

There are many ways of exploring the message of this important new document. There are many themes that can be drawn from it, and different groups and people will want to explore different aspects. However, it would be useful for everyone to become familiar with three of the fundamental ideas that the Pope invites us to consider.

The themes are set out below, and are based on scripture. They can be used both reflectively and as discussion starters.

THEME 1: Based on Scripture

The basic ideas of the document are woven around the scriptural image of the labourers in the vineyard. One way of introducing people to these ideas is through reflection on some of the passages used.

1 **We are all called by the Lord in baptism to be labourers in his vineyard.**

The parable of the labourers in the vineyard (Matthew 20 vv1-6). The call of the Lord to each person is 'You go into my vineyard too'. We are all personally called by the Lord and sent forth with work to do. Like the labourers, we are called in different ways and at different times, to share in the work that needs to be done.
See paragraphs 1, 2, 3, 45.

2 **The vineyard is the whole world which is to be transformed**

The place where we live is the place where we receive our call from God. The actual circumstances of our lives are where we must seek the Kingdom of God. We can't abandon the world; rather we are called to be 'light' and 'salt' wherever we are, transforming the world from within.
Paragraph 15.

3 **I am the vine and you are the branches** (John 15 vv 1-8, 16-17)

The image of the vine and the branches expresses how the whole of our lives is in unity with Christ. Our daily activities are the place of our mission and the way to our holiness. It also helps us to reflect on the kind of relationships we have with each other in the Church. Being part of one vine means we live in communion with each other. This communion means a sharing of life and love and acceptance of mutual need and interdependence.
See paragraphs 8, 9, 17, 22, 27, 59.

4 **I have appointed you to go out and bear fruit**

The essential demand of life in Christ and life in the Church is bearing fruit. Our life and our mission cannot be separated, just as the branches only bear fruit while they are part of the vine. Our holiness comes from our involvement with the world. The fruit we can bear will be in our living to the full the message of the Gospel.
See paragraphs 17, 22, 27, 32, 34, 59.

5 **Good stewards of God's varied grace**
(1 Peter vv 10-11)

We all receive grace in various ways through Baptism and we are called to be 'good stewards' of the grace we are given. We cannot stand back or remain idle when there is work to be done. This stewarding of God's grace takes place in our involvement in society and also in our full participation in ministries, tasks and offices in the life of the Church.
See paragraphs 20, 21, 23, 26, 27.

THEME 2: The Parish: the Church in the neighbourhoods of humanity

1 The parish is the Church in the midst of people, a eucharistic community with a mission. The parish is called to be 'a house of welcome to all and a place of service to all'.
See paragraphs 26, 27.

2 The parish carries out its mission through responding to people's hopes and deepest desires. It should concern itself with the world's problems.
See paragraph 27.

3 There is a need for a greater effort to renew our parishes. We can do this by adapting structures so that the lay faithful share more fully in pastoral activities.
See paragraph 27.

4 We need to foster within parishes, small communities which share the Word of God and express it in love and service.
See paragraph 26.

5 We need a more convinced and extensive development of parish pastoral councils. See paragraph 27.

THEME 3: To live the Gospel - serving the person and society

1 We are called to service and to solidarity. At the heart of this call is the task of awakening people to each other, to mutual human need and communion with each other. See paragraph 36.

2 We have a particular concern for the dignity of human beings and the equality which makes all kinds of discrimination unacceptable.
See paragraph 37.

3 We give special importance to our mission to those who are weak or sick. We need to approach with courage the new ethical problems raised by scientific progress. See paragraph 38.

4 We cannot justify absence from public life; we have a right and duty to participate in public life in order to shape society in justice, and build solidarity. See paragraph 42.

5 In serving the dignity and rights of the individual and the good of the family, we should be at the forefront in working out solutions to the growing problems of unemployment.
See paragraph 43.

Pat Jones
Director of Parish and Adult Formation
Archdiocese of Liverpool

Grail Publications

SIMPLIFIED COUNCIL DOCUMENTS

This is the Church
Grail version of 'Lumen Gentium'. 'This may be regarded as **the** masterpiece of Vatican II'. Read this and find how it enlarges your vision of the Church, the People of God.

This is the Church in the World Today
Grail version of 'Gaudium et Spes'. An essentially 'pastoral' document which is an eye-opener on the role of Christians in today's swiftly changing scene.

This is Religious Freedom
Grail version of 'Dignitatis Humanae'. A good companion to the document on the lay apostolate, included in the same volume. It considers the meaning of true freedom and human dignity.

This is the Liturgy
This is Divine Revelation
Both documents in one volume:
Grail version of 'Sacrosanctum Concilium'. The public worship of Christian people is the Liturgy.Liturgy is always in process of renewal, is always asking Christians for renewed understanding and participation. This helps towards such new vision.

Grail version of 'Dei Verbum'. This is a magnificent document that treats of God's word in Scripture. Many parallels are drawn between liturgy and scripture. This is almost a commentary on the liturgy document.

This is Ecumenism
Eastern Catholic Churches
The Church and non-Christian Religions
Three documents in one volume:
Grail version of 'Unitatis Redintegratio'. A hopeful, realistic document on the nature and development of Christian Unity. 'No Catholic document has ever spoken of non-Catholic Christians in this way.'

Grail version of 'Orientalium Ecclesiarum'. Complements the document on ecumenism. It clarifies the position and rights of Eastern Churches.

Grail version of 'Nostra Aetate'. Affirms that all peoples with their various religions form one community. Splendid treatment of Jewish-Christian relations.

SIMPLIFIED ENCYCLICALS

This is Man Redeemed
Grail version of 'Redemptor Hominis', Pope John Paul II's first encyclical. It stresses the dignity of men and women and their human rights.

This is Human Work
Grail version of 'Laborem Exercens'. Pope John Paul deals with capital and labour, workers' rights and the spiritualisation of work.

This is God's Mercy
Grail version of 'Dives et Misericordia'. In the tensions of today, caused largely by world-wide inequalities, the Church must bear true witness, says John Paul.

WHAT IS THE GRAIL?

The Grail is a Society, part of which is a Secular Institute for women. The Centre is at Pinner, Middlesex.

Staff Members of the Grail are women who live mainly at the Grail Centre experiencing the demands and satisfactions of a secular, non-institutional community life.

Companions of the Grail are members of the Society with an individual mission. They live in their own homes, following their chosen occupation, while having at the same time close regular contact with each other and with Staff Members.

Grail Partners form the third arm of the Grail Society. Membership is open to married couples who are prepared to make a serious commitment to deepen their own personal values and who feel drawn to a close fellowship with other couples according to the Grail Way of Life.

The Grail is well known for its publications (this simplified document 'This is the Laity' being typical); for the courses it runs at the Centre and for its work with families.

The Grail also offers people space for peace and quiet; for others, a chance to reassess their lives either as Short Term Members of the Community or as Volunteers at the Centre.

For further information about the Grail Society and/or its programme of events, write to:
Mary Grasar, The Grail, 125 Waxwell Lane, Pinner, Middx HA5 3ER Tel: 01.866.0505